Sleeping Woman Mountain

Sleeping Woman Mountain

Poems by

Argos MacCallum

Cover design by Shay Culligan
Cover image by Corinna MacNeice

ISBN: 978-1-63980-159-6

Kelsay Books
502 South 1040 East, A-119
American Fork, Utah 84003
Kelsaybooks.com

for Corinna
y todas mis hermanas

Contents

Let my body be as a prayer stick for the earth.
—anonymous

i am the hummingbird at your flower
the leaf in your breeze
the pebble in the desert
and the hole in your sleeve

Arrival

Your shoulders and breasts curve upwards
in the candlelight, a steep smooth horizon.
Through the window mountains loom
in the moonlight, barely visible.

Lying down, I am amazed
that the road was so long,
the earth so old, the hour so young,
and my calculations such beggars
before your smile.

Bilbao

young woman walks in the soft silver morning
on a sidewalk in the sloping neighborhood
near the river banks in Bilbao

a third story window swings open
two young women lean over the sill
wave to the girl on the ground

and call out in melon and mermaid sounds
with a honey rumble of laughter
cooing in a primeval code

the young woman swings around and waves
brushes back her long black hair
sings like chocolate up to the pair

as silk-scarves of a secret intimacy
dangle and dance in the springtime air
in some supple conspiracy of bliss

and the hill became elated
and the sky embraced all
and the earth continued to spin

and spin and spin

Minor Success

A small hut, whitewashed, bed, table and chairs
stare out darkened windows like immigrants.
The small potbelly stove gurgles
in its maiden voyage this season.
A fly, night-watchman of its species,

buzzed by the lamp and fell to the floor.
This hut I built once, but tonight
I am a traveling guest, caught in the immense
chill silver sphere of darkness
on the route to tomorrow.

You dozed in the chair, then crossed to the bed.
The silence was asleep already.
Your beauty awoke, as if the smile you carry
requires too much voltage.

Conversing with your beauty, I found it odd
that I should be an old gentleman
with a tick, thick glasses, and a cane
living so ill at ease
in a dimly remembered novel that once
enjoyed a certain minor success.

6th Grade Girl

sixth grade sock-hop in the gym
prancing fear and a jacket and a tie
turned down twice by some of the girls
it's my broken teeth and glasses and freckles

there's a geiger counter in my chest
chirping in the mad tension piercing this boy
and thinking each song not quite right for asking
again, anymore, ever

until time slips into the last song and a panic
siren sends this boy in a lope tracing
the rim of a constellation of dancing couples
with the deep recesses of space inside his ribs

by some command of deep iron
by an utter urgency of life
I sensed you before I saw you
hard starboard my body swung
through a field of asteroids

my eyes fused with yours
our arms rose in the pulse of surety
the obvious electric rightness of us
and such a sigh of celestial grape-tasting relief
locked in the haven of your slow-dance gravity

Morning Halo

you leaned toward your friend
the rose nymph from the Bay

to show her your silver necklace
of tribal proportions

your right hand rose swiftly
as you leaned forward to catch
an errant collar or indolent lapel
but your blouse had none

and your fingertips landed
on the moon of your right breast

in the shadow of Sleeping Woman Mountain
under the hammers rapping on your roof

The soft shallows became lunar lakes
as the morning sun and expresso
drew haloes around the country
of your sumerian goddess body

lakes crested with gold-edged waves
and the drums calling from above
brought us to the shores
of primal amazement

as innocent and fierce
as the dawn-riding star

Close

Lone woman lives high on a hill
over the river, railroad, and village
in a dilapidated trailer
with a broken front door
closed with a brick and a wire.

Raises a teenage daughter in school
waitresses at night
studies in the day for a degree
sews for extra money, lives
close to the edge.

Though I'll never win her proud love
I hung a door I made in the rickety frame
when she wasn't home. It'll keep
out the wind, but when I finished,
I was close to tears.

She'll offer to pay me but as a friend
and carpenter I have my reward.
I did what I could, and only hope
as she steps through this door others
might close and open.

Ioannis' Song

Sunrise caught the white hollyhock
in the sidereal splendor of unfurling
its silken starlight wings
in a counter-clockwise sweep
of galactic gypsy trails

and startled in the act
of her magic incantation
she withdrew to her green core
her wings locked and stilled
in the brass light

oh hollyhock
sibling of the sparkling stars
shy sister of my beloved
calling card of the angels
sensual and sublime

my beloved will hurry
to bring you a dew of diamonds
and the nectar of apple
a smile of a mountain rim
and tears of the wind

stand with us hollyhock
in the morning storm of pearls
funnel the solar winds
into flutes of greensong
grant this boon handmaid of the moon

my beloved stands clothed in sun
as hummingbirds flock to her nipples
let us post our cunning joy
in care of the messenger clouds
to the random countries of sighs

and as my beloved so prayed
the passage of nights
suckled the white spiral
with the brine of the moon
into a trumpet of triumph

Autumn

fifty years ago
on a red-aired day in the apple of autumn
as classmates whirl about in recess
a boy of just-six stands in the scrabble of a school-yard
stilled in a place with its separate light and color
held in a gasp without time

across the fence line and clusters of tumbleweed
just past the village library and fire station
under the flames of the towering cottonwoods
his mother on her knees refinishes a prized table
in the bare yard between the adobe house
and the chicken coops

her red hair dances in the giddy breeze
as her long thin arms glide over the wood
intent on her work the playground babble
mingles with the staccato of the rattling leaves
as the gold hues of October shimmer
around her

her son just recovered from a long illness
and behind in school (can't add twelve and twelve)
and suddenly again on his own away from home
sees her
and discovers a trust that powers the world
the drums of life calling over the distance
connecting a young mother and a young son
like stars of a constellation

Love Poem

Your fingers circle my waist
like Orion's belt
bracing my back
for the madness I undertake

Ivory and chocolate
the earth in your eyes
lemon laugh and saffron smile
tether my spirit until sunrise

I came empty-handed
ashamed before your simple riches
my purse has only a beggar's dream
you give me back love and sandwiches

In the meridian of my life
I saw you sitting at a dance
one song led to another
two chords knotted in romance

Forgive me if I drift
forgive me if I fall into dreams
yours is the light which brings me home
from the dark wilderness I roam

Summer Rain

The grey sky clamps to the horizon
hiding the mountains. Only close hills
sit in light. The long night of rain coats
the tall summer grass. The barn never looked better,
shining in dark water silhouette
framed in the fog. Today this desert
looks like somewhere east.

Last night the tall shock of air and thunder
gave way to fans of water, like
a name called gently,
a young boy's hand reaching
up for a father.

Coracle

silhouettes of passersby ghost past the picket fence
the songbird sleeps in the tree
the last reveler hurtles past in a mass of metal
and the melon moon waltzes graciously

a luminous bed on a maiden voyage
slips its mooring of eastern smiles
and sails into the phoenix hours
two pilgrims cradled in a coracle

buoyed on the symphony of swirling water
eddies of caresses and deep pools of wine
slender fingers learn new navigation
in a hibiscus of kisses like splashes of rain

Fan the Sky

an incense of dust hovers in the roadway
mingling with an old moon-smile of moisture
from the gentle acequia

dry tumbleweed grapples with the barbwire
remnants of pocked sun-bleached newspaper
cling to the spikes and barbs

my father stands in the yard
under the epoch of cottonwoods
in a collusion of centuries

in front of the mud-plastered casita
in the center of the village
next to the fire station and general store

three young sons revolve at his feet
—the eldest just attending school—
taunting the tumbleweed with sticks

he extracts a swatch of newspaper
from its grapple hooks on the fence
as red dust rises through the odors of apples

and scrutinizes the withering messages
the smatter of dissolving print
while clicking his tongue like a crow

as the son in school looks up at him
towering in the red-rayed twilight
with a widening pride and an awe

and a lesson on how to read the world
which is now disappearing in the dusk
as tail-feathers of the falling red sun

fan the sky

April

the dead piñon is a whirling dervish
whirling so fast   it is so still
so slow in the sideways of time

as an owl cries in the dusk
of a rain-drunk April
the young sun has fingers

that coax me to the edge
of mind and mindlessness
with erotic pinches

Bobbie Burns Night

after the Bobbie Burns night

    the shrike of bagpipes in the whisky air
    the haggis and the swarm of kilts

as nimble giants danced like tides
around their stalwart women

our highland home was far away
our lowland relatives begged us to stay

the air crackled in the skipping night
the fog bulldogged the tires

    eddies of neon rippled past
    like minnows and the wind

the wind guffawed at the street signs

our highland home was far away
the coaxing cold begged us to stay

the long road crept toward midnight
and several stars beyond

    we skirled through the gloom
    and a bird goddess guided us

as clouds and hills tumbled behind

our highland home was far away
the wayside abysses begged us to stay

we burst into a ring of mountains
the tall tankards of the highlands

    shimmering in the maddened air
    as snow gyres romped around us

and flails of ice snapped in delight

our highland home was far away
the jaws of snow begged us to stay

the road slowed to a trickle
and time followed suit

    with a rudder of forged love
    we shoaled through the deep

and the vast trembling nighttime
and the last and swooning sleep

    yet we shared the elixir of danger
    and yes too the nectar of life

as we synchronized our pirouettes
with the cat-dance drifts of white

our highland home was far away
the silky snow nymphs begged us to stay

at the umbilical of our homestead
on the skirt of our sovereign Hill

    we ran aground on a reef of snow
    in an immense shudder of stillness

with a headlong mile to go

our highland home was far away
a milky way of snowflakes begged us to stay

the road and the fences had all lain down
beneath the powdered confection

    we tugged on our scarves
    and headed instead across the crust

in a generally western direction

our highland home was far away
the night-capped junipers begged us to stay

we rose and fell in the swelling waves
bobbing up to our belts in laughter

    the stupendous darkness and the singeing wind
    cat-called and each step was a prayer

each breath a wish for home and lair

our highland home was far away
the arctic lullabies begged us to stay

like a sunrise on Mars we saw light afar
and headed for the shores of safety

    the door hinges heralded us hoarsely
    we stamped the snow   stood our coats

in the corner and called for the kettle to crow

and under the covers in a riot of limbs
we struck fire in our hearth of hearts

    with gasps and giggles groans and growls
    in a tumult of praise for the fierce wee world

for all of the grave and for all of the quick

sigh might shatter

hope the sun warmed you this afternoon
with the gold leaf of november's embers
for the silver night of the huntress moon
promises a silence so taut
a sigh might shatter it into sea-foam
and sparkles that covet
the diamonds of your eyes

Maiden

Mérida
mi hermana

lady of the tea
chocolate smile
and honeycomb
of wise woman's wrinkles

the deep coals of your heart
would fuel a crucible of love
would transform the coursing pain
into trefoils of apricot sun

your heart springs on goat hooves
on the sea cliff of la isla
sails the arroyos of enchantment
in a galleon of wishes
clamors the dew-bristling apple trees
in the green billowing hills of britain

could I have witnessed your nimble rise
to take the hand to dance the dance of death
your shout of bliss still a foghorn in the storm

I carry a locket of your bird rising to wing
the swivel of your red dress rising from the chair
while butterflies launched from your eyes
and your lips arched in moon crescent and hollyhock

when I first met you at a dance in our waning youth
in a swarthy brown July dusk
the primitive prophecy
of the July of your green disappearance

oh sister in the dimming light
let your sonnet tackle tears
your fingers sieve the beads of silence
let a rainbow traipse about you
and the mist of sea mountains
flatter your feet

Afternoon

Do the orange flowers grow quickly
after your footsteps? Dark clouds dash
to your drawing board, and lucky
raindrops aim for your watercup?

Don't try to persuade me it isn't so.
I see what the sun does when
left alone with you.
The trees can't hide

your red hair with their curtains
of green. And besides,
I still see you after you disappear.
Because your smile is the knife point

piercing the melon, your eyes
the jarring dive of the nighthawk,
your movements a stream slaking thirst,
your fingers hoofbeats over my heart.

Iridescent

your jade girl eyes are opaque
yet glisten
in the chalice of western light
the second sickle moon hovers above
the throat of Sleeping Woman Mountain

robed in leopard skin
you swayed in the doorway
of days to come

a morning later the western hills
stood iridescent
in the burnished copper light of the east
under a rainbow arched proud of the heavens

just before the smudged clouds
and absent-minded drizzles
suckled the land all day long

Setting Sail

for Celeste

cat straddles the stoop
mists mask the mountain
the raven pony-rides the juniper
the aloe and the cholla sigh

the rain and the cornmeal
gather in the feast of the day
the jackdaw lightning and the thunder bassoon
the kettle the candle the wooden spoon

your love moves like a sacred serpent
divine and mesmerizingly primeval
the birthright of all beings is love
the cat licks its tail

the cave the castle the kitchen cupboard
simple supper and the fragrance of patience
your orphaned shadow whispers in my ear
the willow tree sheds a crystal tear

native matron fountain of joy
set sail on the lure of the sea
the waves of the purple summer sky
and the magic map of your seismic embrace

bedrock

the sky rained on my notebook
through the open window
raising mountain ranges on the pages
reaching deep down through layers
of porphyry and proto-poetry
down to the first bedrock metaphor
the first wink of the muse

I glance and glance
at my japanese classmate
as her pen strokes the paper
in our third-grade poetry hour
and I secretly send my invisible words
to her on that young february afternoon
with the brave motes that danced

in the white gold sunlight
streaming through the windows
through my heart
and her silk black hair hung straight down
waving to roots underground
and I knew I had been alive before
because beauty of trust and trust of beauty

are one and the same

Chasm

The sinuous Spanish singer
with coils of hair similar to the sun in color
wrapped in the rhythm of burnished silk
flings her fingers high on the rising surf of her breath
coaxing upward a firestorm of flamenco
from the fire-pit of her hips

and up in the light booth of the theater
mesmerized I can see clearly down
the golden ruby chasm of her throat
and straight into the soul of her heart

           **

The goose on the nest in the goose-house
white one-year-old fragile and ferocious
ensconced in straw with a single
newborn gosling under her wing
looks up to my peeping head in the doorway
and screams a heart-bending warning call

and in the calm of a golden morning
mesmerized I can see clearly down
the golden ruby chasm of her throat
and straight into the soul of her heart

           **

The full moon falls into the throat
of Sleeping Woman Mountain
as daylight urges bees
to the throats of apple blossoms
the coy cat releases a plaintive meow
and I'm already falling
into the golden ruby chasm of your kisses

10th Grade Girl

your black eyes and the purple half-moons beneath them
your black eyes burned with the ferocity of a lion
and the yearning of a hummingbird

your face against the car window
begging your parents to stop
and offer this boy a ride to school

on the edge of the back seat
your late spring hunger throbbed at me
and you devoured all the oxygen around us

sweet desert-star jewish girl
trembling in the newness of your full woman's body
you showed me my hunger mirrored so hugely in yours

this boy untutored in the power of such magnetic storms
paralyzed by clanging bells inside and the lurching car
and the frowns of the father

he was caught on both horns of fear and landed
very far away trying to avoid you
until his family and he left town

had one kiss flowered that day the world began
we might have graced ourselves with fledgling wings
to begin mapping the vast terrain of the world of love

Drought-slayer

drought-slayer
    finger-paint the sky with your arsenal of blues
    let your thumb map the spikes of lightning
    may you ignite the air
    with the crazed and cutting aroma of rain
    and signal the wind to sweet-wail
    like the smoke from a submerged horn

    and may my love lie with me
    in the hammock of the sunset
    to see bursting diamonds in the sky
    between the slow gallop of buffalo clouds
    and hear the sacred timpani of water falling
    on the murmuring earth

drought-slayer
    my heart depends on you

san francisco sea nymph

In the sea air of san francisco
misted night shadows down to the sea
the newspaper boy slaloms
in his wet roman sandals
weaving through obsidian colored streets
in a big bump of hills
in the first hint of dawn
and leaves the rolled-up world
at certain front doors
of the colored stuccoed houses
leaning on each other's shoulders
drunkenly plumb in descent to the sea

and crossing through the moon-fed luminescence
of a tilted intersection
as rain drops crackled in the air
the newspaper boy slithers up a flight of stairs
to set the paper by the somnolent front door
and descends into the surprise
of a sinewy sea nymph
at the side door downstairs
who commands silence and a nimble slip
into a tented loft in the garage
bangles and sequins gleam on the wall
and satin pillows undulate and preen

my wet feet and her earnest eyes
and a sputtering fire in between
she kissed me first
for I knew not how
in the hallowed lair of a mermaid

but she learned me well
and kept it to kisses
for a novice will ignite with too many wishes
colors swam in the air above where we lay
and the twilight refused to yield to the day

and later out in the green sauce of morning
as the streetlights winked and disappeared
the peninsula began to pulse with steel and shouts
and sunbeams swiveled through the clouds
the newspaper boy delivered
the last of his rolled-up worlds
late and belated and dazed and amazed
as his heart careened around the rink of his ribs
and he never forgot the sea nymph
until his dying day

An Allowance of Grace

In the throes of the thunderstorm
clothed only in stillness
we stood side by side
in the house we built
from scratch and love
peering through the plate glass
as if on the bridge of a ship
before the dark waves
of the exploding heavens

yet the eyes of the storm
were within our hearts
for an uncanny calm
caressed us in our cradle cave
the black clouds ballooned above us
the trees yanked and stretched their tethers
and the usual mountains
in their ring of alliance
were nowhere to be seen

and in the eon of an instant
between us there appeared
a slender cylinder of diamond light
pure exact stalactite
a sliver of lightning
a shimmering platinum lily
which fused our hearts
together forever

we looked in each other eyes
and through an allowance of grace
glimpsed the beginning of time

an actual occurrence of cylindrical ball lightning in our house, 2007

Waterbone

the dark owl hoots in the horse chestnut tree
the glitter of stars falls like rain
spoke of geese skims through the high night of winter

beads of water slide past the breastbone

let me come to you as a bird
bluejay perched on silver moonlight
roadrunner crossing six lanes in a dusk of dreams

beads of water run past the breastbone

a stammer of crows gargle morning news
nighthawk cleaves the jigsaw of junipers
raven tap-dances on a telephone pole

beads of water roll past the breastbone

hummingbird nuzzles the geranium
magpie beats the drum
grosbeak surveys terrain

beads of water glide past the breastbone

a red gate and purple lilac and black cat
your smile like the curve of the earth
a nest in an abyss of bliss

beads of water cartwheel past the breastbone

Three Sons

Three sons
in an old panel wagon
the words "ice cream"
hand-painted on the hood
inch down a one-way street
in rush-hour traffic
a regulation cardboard casket (oversized)
their mother inside
headed for the crematorium
two candles on the floor
flicker steadily by her head
a pine bough and an eagle feather
a bottle of scotch for the boys

The little man in a three-piece suit
waits after closing time
with a little trolley and papers to sign
(the money paid in advance)
on that snowy January day

forever and once ago.

Trellis

for Cather

The blue flowers on the table heard us
talking softly on Sunday, catching our murmurs
like a dew of nourishing tears,
or perhaps our own thoughts which we didn't hear.

Born of a summer serenity,
cut and arranged in a passage
through which the changes of autumn walk
with a rosary of what the world was and will be.

Robed in the same blue flames of slender strength
you sat in the autumn light
bearing those changes in the seasons of your life
bearing the taxing pain with a calm-laced grace.

Yet with roots in a soil of memories
the succeeding moments when you succeeded and
will succeed
supported by a trellis of friends, and a future
of unforetold flowerings.

About the Author

Argos MacCallum has lived in Santa Fe since 1967, and has worked as a carpenter, plasterer, ranch manager, orchardist, furniture-maker, scene shop manager, as well as a film and stage actor and stage director. His chapbook, *She Loved Gravity and Would Fall Down Exquisitely Anywhere,* was published in 1987. He has worked with many theatre companies in Santa Fe, and is an artistic director and co-founder of Teatro Paraguas, a bilingual theatre promoting contemporary Latinx theatre, children's theatre, New Mexico playwrights, and poetry readings since 2004.

His poems have been published in *Malpais Review, Lummox Anthology, PoetryXHunger.com, THE Magazine, wildword.net,* and *Poetry London/Apple Magazin*e.

www.ingramcontent.com/pod-product-compliance
Lightning Source LLC
Chambersburg PA
CBHW030814090426
42737CB00010B/1277